Vegan Cookbook for Beginners

Easy & Healthy Recipes to Get Started

By Maya Perry

Table of Contents

INTRODUCTION

Contrary to some opinions, eating a vegan diet doesn't have to feel restrictive, boring, or mundane! In fact, eating healthy has never been so easy or so delicious. Thanks to modern technology, many people have access to a wide variety of healthy, animal-free, nutrient-rich foods at all times of the year, providing a rich basis for expanding one's palate and enjoying a cruelty-free lifestyle. The exciting, healthy, and delicious recipes in this cookbook support a vegan lifestyle and provide a great resource for everything from quick-and-easy meals to tasty dishes to serve friends and family.

A common concern of those investigating the vegan lifestyle is getting adequate nutrition. The truth is, every approach to eating requires some conscientious thought to ensure that you get all of the nutrients that your body needs to thrive, and veganism is no different. You will need to make sure that you are getting enough healthy fats, vitamins, iron, and protein. In most cases, these needs can be met through simple planning. When done right, a vegan diet is healthy and nutritious. It also provides many other benefits, including:

- *Health Benefits.* Vegan diets are usually rich in fiber and nutrients such as folic acids, magnesium, and phytochemicals, as well as many vitamins and healthy fats. The healthy fruits, vegetables, and whole grains common to vegan diets, in combination with a natural reduction in processed foods and animal products, have the power to lower your risk of obesity, heart disease, cancer, and diabetes.
- *Environmentally Friendly.* A vegan diet has the potential to reduce our personal environmental footprint, because it doesn't rely on the high-impact farming practices that are one of the many downsides of a

meat-eating economy. Not all vegetable farming represents a lower environmental impact, but many do. Thoughtfully choosing which vegetables to include in your diet can help support the environment.

- *Cruelty-free.* Vegan diets allow us to eat healthy, delicious meals that don't come at the cost of other animals, whether that be a cost in lives or in suffering and cruelty.

Principles of Vegan Eating

Veganism is different from vegetarianism in that a vegan diet abstains completely from the consumption of animal products. This includes eggs, dairy, meat, and honey as well as animal byproducts such as gelatin and carmine. A vegan lifestyle also includes abstaining from the use of non-food animal products such as leather, fur, and ivory. However, in this cookbook we will of course be focusing primarily on the dietary aspects of a vegan lifestyle.

Tips for Optimal Nutrition

It's important to ensure that you are getting enough nutrition when eating a vegan diet. Keep the following 5 tips in mind as you plan your meals:

- *Eat a variety of foods.* Don't get stuck in just a handful of your favorite vegetables to eat and prepare. Instead, get better nutritional coverage by eating a variety of fruits, vegetables, nuts, seeds, legumes, and grains.
- *Get enough protein.* Make sure to know how much protein your body needs for your age, height, weight, and physical activity level. Plan your meals so that you are able to meet your daily protein requirements with

protein-rich vegetables, nuts, seeds, legumes. Avoid overconsumption of processed faux meats, as these often contain preservatives, food dyes, and excess sodium. Whenever possible, take your protein from whole-food sources.

- *Get enough Omega-3s.* Make sure to include healthy oils and foods with this important nutrient in your diet. If you take an omega-3 supplement, make sure that you know what it's made from. Fish oil is one of the most common sources of omega-3s in supplements, which can be problematic for vegans. Good food sources of Omega-3s include coconut oil, avocados, and many nuts and seeds.

- *Get enough vitamins.* Don't assume that because you're eating a lot of fruits and vegetables, you must be getting all of the vitamins that you need. Educate yourself on potential tough spots for and make sure to include foods in your diet that contain these nutrients in adequate amounts. You may also want to consider taking a quality multivitamin to help keep your bases covered. However, you should never use supplements as a replacement for food-based nutrition. Also, make sure to read labels carefully to ensure that are no animal products in the vitamin capsules.

- *Choose your salts.* Not all salts are created equal. You may want to consider using a Himalayan pink salt rather than your standard table salt as this salt has been reported to contain a number of important minerals. However, more research needs to be done in this area, so think carefully before choosing a salt for regular consumption. Whichever salt you choose, make sure that you are getting enough salt without straying into the realm of too much.

Prep Time

Most of the recipes in this book can be prepared in under 30 minutes. To further reduce prep time, consider planning your meals a week ahead of time. That way, you can prep more time-consuming items in advance and have them ready on the day of the meal that needs them. For example, if you know you will be having a recipe that requires quinoa on Monday and again on Thursday, you can save time by making enough quinoa on Monday to cover both recipes. You can also wash and chop many vegetables a couple of days in advance. It's also helpful to prepare vegan snacks and divide them up in individual bags or containers for easy access throughout the week.

Vegan Cheese

Yes, it's surprisingly easy to give up real cheese and substitute it with nutritious soya-based and nut-based cheese. You can buy any of the non-diary vegan cheeses on the market or just cook it yourself! Healthy and delicious either used as a gourmet ingredient for a salad or just spread grilled onto sandwiches, stuffed in vegan wraps, or even served as a great appetizer on its own. Enjoy!

Vegan Zucchini Cheese

Preparation time: 20 minutes
Cooking time: 2 hours

Ingredients for 4 portions:

2 zucchini, medium size, sliced
2 onions, minced
2 tbsp. agar-agar
1 tbsp. garlic powder
1 tbsp. lemon juice
1 tbsp. salt

Directions:

Lay parchment or wax paper (any cheesecloth) in a baking
pan. Bring sliced zucchini to a boil, then reduce heat to
simmer. Allow zucchini to simmer for 10 minutes more to
soften. Remove from heat and let cool slightly.

Place zucchini in a food processor (or blender) mixed with
onion, garlic powder and lemon juice.
Add agar-agar and blend thoroughly.

Place the mass into the baking pan and place in a refrigerator
until your cheese is chilled and solid. Serve on a burger or in
any Italian dish.

Tip: If kept for a week in a fridge, this cheese will firmer and
stay together better.

Vegan Mozzarella Cheese

Preparation time: 10 minutes
Cooking time: 2 hours

Ingredients for 4 portions:

1/2 cup raw cashews, soaked in hot water for 30 minutes
1 cup hot water
3 tbsp. tapioca starch
1 tbsp. nutritional yeast
1 tsp. apple cider vinegar
1/2 tsp. salt
1/4 tsp. onion powder
1/4 tsp. garlic powder
1/8 tsp. white pepper

Directions:

Drain and rinse the cashews and place them in a blender with the rest of the ingredients. Blend until smooth. Transfer to a saucepan, stirring the cheese constantly. After 1-2 minutes, the cheese will start to get thick. Keep stirring until cheese begins to move together while stirring. Remove from heat and let cool. Refrigerate for 2 hours or more.

Vegan Tofu Feta Cheese

Preparation time: 20 minutes
Cooking time: 2 hours

Ingredients for 4 portions:

9.7 oz. firm tofu
1/2 cup water
1/2 cup apple cider vinegar
1/4 cup lemon juice
1 tbsp. oregano, dry

Directions:

Cut the ready tofu into cubes. Mix all the marinade ingredients in a container. Add the tofu, mix together with the lemon juice, apple cider vinegar, water and oregano. Place in the fridge for approx. 2 hours.

Tip: This cheese is ready to be served immediately, but it is better after 2 days of refrigeration.

Homemade Vegan Sour Cream

Preparation time: 10 minutes
Cooking time: 2 hours

Ingredients for 4 portions:

1½ cups raw cashews, soaked
3/4 cup water
2 tbsp. apple cider vinegar
2 tbsp. lemon juice, fresh,
1/2 tbsp. salt

Directions:

Cover the cashews with cool water in a cooking bowl and let soak for 8 hours, or pour boiling water over the cashews and soak for 1 hour. Rinse and drain.

Place the cashews into a food processor or a blender (high-speed). Add the water, lemon, vinegar and salt and blend the mass until smooth. Add some more water if needed to get it going better. Place the mass into a container and chill in the fridge to thicken. This cheese can be kept for up to one week in a fridge.

Tip: You can freeze this cheese and keep up to a month.

Vegan Parmesan Cheese

Preparation time: 10 minutes
Cooking time: 2 hours

Ingredients for 4 portions:

1/4 cup nutritional yeast
1/2 cup almonds, blanched and slivered
1/2 cashews, raw
1/4 tsp. garlic powder
1/2 tsp. salt

Directions:

Mix all the ingredients in the bowl of a food processor or a blender (fitted with "S" blade). Mix until the mass is finely smooth. Place it into the fridge. Serve at least 2 hours later. Can be kept in a fridge up to 2 months.

Basic Vegan Almond Cheese

Preparation time: 10 minutes
Cooking time: 6 hours+

Ingredients for 4 portions:

5.5 oz. almonds, blanched, soaked for 5 hours (or overnight)
2/3 cup water
2 – 3 tbsp. lemon juice
1/2 clove garlic
3 tbsp. olive oil
1¼ tbsp. salt
herbs to liking
1/4 cup nutritional yeast, or to liking

Directions:

After the almonds are soaked, drain them and place into a blender with water, lemon juice, olive oil, garlic and salt. Blend until smooth. Lay a cheesecloth into the bowl and place the mixture on top of it. Keep in a fridge for several hours to remove excess water.

After the mixture has drained well, invert it onto a baking sheet brushed with olive oil. Remove all of the cheesecloth. Bake 25-30 (350°F/180°C) minutes for a spreadable meal or 30-40 minutes (350°F/180°C) for a firm, but still creamy cheese. You can bake it longer for a sliceable cheese. Serve chilled.

Tip: Use ground almonds instead of the whole or slivered and you will blend immediately without soaking.

Summer Mix Salad

Preparation time: 10 minutes

Ingredients for 4 portions:

6 leaves of Romaine Lettuce, torn
6 cherry tomatoes, halved or quartered
1 carrot, grated
1/2 red onion, chopped
1 seedless cucumber (optional)
1 pack seasoned bread croutons (optional)
handful of toasted almonds/pine nuts/walnuts (any)
cranberries for garnish, dried

Dressing:

1 tbsp. distilled vinegar or lime juice
1 tsp Dijon mustard
1 tbsp. honey

2 tbsp. extra-virgin olive oil
pinch of salt, as per taste
1 tsp black pepper, freshly ground

Directions:

Mix all the salad ingredients except nuts and croutons in a large bowl. Prepare the dressing by first adding Dijon mustard to vinegar or juice and whisking well. Add freshly ground black pepper, salt, and honey; mix well. Whisk vigorously while adding extra-virgin olive oil. Spread over the salad, mix, and cover it with plastic wrap. Keep refrigerated. When ready to eat, top with toasted almonds and croutons.

Tip: For crunchy salad, wash the greens and use a salad spinner to remove excess water, or you can dab excess water from the leaves with a kitchen towel.

Roasted Beetroot and Pumpkin Salad

Preparation time: 15 minutes

Ingredients for 4 portions:

1 lb. pumpkin, deseeded and chopped into 1/2-inch cubes
1 lb. fresh beetroot, cut into 1/2-inch cubes

4 slices of grilled Vegan Mozzarella cheese (please see our version of Mozzarella Cheese in the Vegan Cheese Recipes part of this book)
2 tbsp. olive oil
2 tbsp. fresh basil leaves, shredded
sea salt and black pepper to season

Directions:

Preheat oven to 350°F/180°C. In a baking dish, combine pumpkin, onion, beetroot and olive oil. Add sea salt and pepper to taste. Roast for 60 minutes until pumpkin is golden and starting to caramelize, and beetroot is cooked through. Put the cheese slices into the grill oven for 2 minutes and apply atop of each serving. Top with basil and toss gently.

Beetroot and Lentils Salad

Preparation time: 15 minutes

Ingredients for 4 portions:

1 bunch beetroot, scrubbed, trimmed and halved if large
1 tbsp. cumin seeds
1 tbsp. red wine vinegar
1 clove garlic, crushed
1 tsp Dijon mustard
1 oz. pack fresh mint, leaves only, chopped
7 oz. lentils
1 small red onion, finely sliced
2 ripe pears, cored and cubed
4 oz. pack watercress, stalks removed
5 oz. Vegan Tofu Feta cheese, diced (please see our version
of this cheese in the Vegan Cheese recipes part of this book)
4 tbsp. extra virgin olive oil
salt and pepper, to taste

Directions:

Preheat the oven to 390°F/200°C. Place the beetroot in a
roasting tin. Toss with 1 tbsp. of the oil and the cumin seeds,
then roast for about 35-45 minutes until tender. In a large
bowl, whisk together the remaining oil, vinegar, garlic,
mustard, mint and seasoning. Meanwhile, place the lentils in a
pan and cover with cold water. Bring to a boil then reduce
heat and simmer for 20 minutes until tender. Drain thoroughly,
then add to the dressing and toss together.
Remove the beetroot from the oven and cut into bite-size
chunks. Add to the lentils and leave to cool to room
temperature.
Add the red onion, pears and mixed seeds to the salad and
toss to combine. Serve piled onto the watercress. Also, great
with Vegan Tofu Feta diced or shredded (ready from the
market or homemade) and scattered over the top.

Potato Salad

Preparation time: 15 minutes

Ingredients for 4 portions:

3/4 pound fingerling potatoes
1 tbsp. olive oil
1/4 tsp. grated lemon rind
1 tbsp. lemon juice
1 tsp. Dijon
1/4 tsp. pepper
1/3 cup arugula, chopped
2 tbsp. Kalamata olives, sliced
1 tbsp. parsley, chopped
1 tbsp. fresh basil leaves, chopped
1 tbsp. fresh chives, chopped

Directions:

Place a saucepan filled two-thirds with water over high heat.
Cut potatoes into 1-inch pieces. Add potatoes to pan, cover,

and bring to a boil. Reduce heat to medium-high; cook 5 minutes or until tender. Drain.

Whisk together olive oil, lemon rind, lemon juice, Dijon, and pepper in a bowl. Stir in arugula, Kalamata olives, parsley, basil, and chives. Add drained potatoes; toss gently to coat.

Quinoa Salad

Preparation time: 10 minutes

Ingredients for 4 portions:

Dressing:

1/4 cup lemon juice
2 cloves garlic, minced
2 tbsp. honey
1 tbsp. pomegranate molasses
1/4 cup olive oil
salt and pepper, to taste

Salad:

3 cups cooked quinoa
1½ cups cucumber slices (halves or quarters)
10 oz. cherry or grape tomatoes, cut in half
1/3 cup parsley, chopped
1/3 cup Tofu Feta Cheese, crumbled (please view our easy recipe for Vegan Tofu Feta Cheese)

Directions:

Dressing: Combine the lemon juice, garlic, honey, pomegranate molasses, and a pinch of salt and pepper in a small bowl. Whisk in the olive oil until the dressing is combined. Check for seasonings and adjust as desired.
Salad: In a large bowl, toss together the quinoa, cucumber slices, tomatoes, parsley, and crumbled Vegan Tofu Feta. Add the dressing when ready to serve and toss to combine.

Caprese Salad

Preparation time: 10 minutes

Ingredients for 4 portions:

4-5 cups grape or cherry tomatoes
1 lb. fresh Vegan Mozzarella Cheese (please follow our version of this cheese in the Vegan Cheese recipes section of this book)
1 tbsp. balsamic vinegar or red wine vinegar for a milder flavor
10 - 15 large fresh basil leaves, to taste
4 tbsp. of olive oil
Italian sea salt, to taste
black pepper, to taste, freshly ground

Directions:

Slice tomatoes into halves. Cut Vegan Mozzarella into 1/4 – 1/2-inch cubes. Toss together the tomatoes, Vegan Mozzarella, olive oil, and balsamic vinegar. Tear the basil into large pieces and toss into the salad. Season to taste with sea salt and freshly ground black pepper. Serve immediately (can also be refrigerated to serve a little bit later).

Tip: Serve with fresh, crusty Italian bread

Zucchini and Vegan Mozzarella Salad

Preparation time: 10 minutes

Ingredients for 4 portions:

1 zucchini, spiralized
1 yellow summer squash, spiralized
20 cherry/grape tomatoes, halved
4 oz. fresh homemade Vegan Mozzarella cheese (please find our version of this cheese in the Vegan Cheese Recipes section of this book)

Lemon Basil Vinaigrette:

2 tbsp. lemon juice
2 tbsp. extra virgin olive oil
2 tbsp. white wine vinegar
10 basil leaves, fresh
salt and pepper, to taste

Directions:

Combine lemon juice, extra virgin olive oil, white wine vinegar, fresh basil leaves, and salt and pepper to taste in a blender or food processor until smooth. Divide the squash evenly among bowls with 5 halved cherry tomatoes and 1 oz. fresh Vegan Mozzarella.

Serve each salad with about 2 tablespoons of the lemon basil dressing.

Chick Pea Salad

Preparation time: 20 minutes

Ingredients for 4 portions:

15-oz. can chickpeas, drained
1 clove garlic, minced

1/3 cup or more Vegan Parmesan Cheese, grated (please find our version of this cheese in the Vegan Cheese Recipes section of this book)
2 tbsp. lemon juice
2 tbsp. parsley, fresh and chopped
4 tbsp. olive oil
salt and pepper, to liking

Directions:

Mix the drained chickpeas, basil, parsley, lemon juice, olive oil, and garlic in a bowl. Add some Vegan Parmesan Cheese and toss gently. Add some salt and pepper if needed. Serve chilled or approximately at room temperature.
Tip: Chickpea salad can be cooked ahead.

Red Beets Salad

Preparation time: 40 minutes

Ingredients for 4 portions:

2½ lbs. red beets, roasted
1 onion, finely sliced
1/4 cup olive oil
2 tbsp. vinegar
any herbs, to liking
2 tbsp. Dijon mustard, for flavor
salt and pepper, to taste

Directions:

You can either use ready cooked canned beets from the market or roast the beets yourself. For roasting, clean the beets without peeling them, remove all the leaves, and bake them in a baking dish covered with foil for 45 minutes to 2 hours. When ready (easily tested by a knife or a fork after 45 minutes or so), remove knobs and tails from the roasted beets and peel off skins. As the beets tend to stain anything, peel them gently with a cooking towel or with bare fingers under the cold running water.

Cut beets into 1/2-inch square cubes and place in a salad bowl. Add red onion slices to the bowl. Whisk together olive oil, vinegar, salt, pepper and cumin. Pour mixture over the onions and beets. Stir gently until beets and onions are evenly coated with the oil mixture. Add more salt and pepper to taste, if desired. Marinate for 1 hour at room temperature, then serve.

Avocado & Tofu Feta Salad

Preparation time: 40 minutes

Ingredients for 4 portions:

1 can chickpeas, drained
2 avocados, diced
1 small onion, finely sliced
1/3 cup parsley, chopped
1/3 cup Vegan Tofu Feta Cheese (please find our version of this cheese in the Vegan Cheese Recipes section of this book)
3-4 tbsp. olive oil
1 lime, juiced
salt and pepper, to taste

Directions:
Mix all ingredients in a bowl and stir gently so as not to mash the avocados and Tofu Feta Cheese cubes. Add some salt and pepper if you wish and serve immediately.

Sprouted Grain Salad

Preparation time: 40 minutes

Ingredients for 4 portions:

3 cups grain sprouts
1 large onion, finely sliced
10 cherry tomatoes, fresh
1/2 cup parsley, fresh
1 clove garlic
3 tbsp. lemon juice
4 tbsp. olive oil
1 tbsp. Dijon mustard, for flavor
salt and pepper, to taste

Directions:

For grain sprouts: Although it can be kept further in a fridge, the most effective and healthy sprouted grain is freshly cooked and served immediately. To prepare the sprouts you will need to wash the grain thoroughly several times and then place it onto a dish or bowl with water covering the grain for at least a day (3 days maximum).

Combine the sprouts, onion, tomatoes and parsley. Add the dressing ingredients and the salad in a bowl then toss to combine. Serve immediately.

Tip: Vegetable ingredients can be changed as you may like.

Zucchini wraps

Preparation time: 40 minutes

Ingredients for 4 portions:

2 zucchini, finely sliced lengthwise
4 oz. rice, uncooked
1 cup Vegan Parmesan cheese, grated (please find our version of this cheese in the Vegan Cheese Recipes section of this book)

1/2 cup of milk, to taste
2 tbsp. lemon juice
1 tbsp. olive oil
1 pinch of parsley or basil or any fresh herb to taste
salt and pepper, freshly ground, to taste

Directions:

Bring the rice to a boil, add some salt and pepper to taste. Mix
with Vegan Parmesan cheese when ready. Make a layer of 3
long zucchini slices each, laying the slices on top of each
other and thus forming a circle.
Place 1/4 of your Creamy Vegan Parmesan rice filling onto the
zucchini layer and wrap it. Make 4 portions using all the
ingredients.

Sprinkle the zucchini wraps with olive oil and lemon juice,
place them into the oven at medium heat and bake for 10
minutes. Serve warm with a pinch of the fresh herbs on top.

Dried Tomatoes

Preparation time: 40 minutes

Ingredients for 4 portions:

1 large yellow onion, finely chopped
2 cloves garlic, minced
10 oz. cut sun-dried tomatoes with herbs in oil, drained
1½ cups water
6 oz. tomato paste
1/2 tbsp. dried thyme
1/4 cup red wine vinegar
4 tbsp. olive oil
1 tbsp. balsamic vinegar, to liking
salt and pepper, to taste

Directions:

Heat the oil in a saucepan and then add the onion and garlic. Stir until soft and lightly brown. Add the dried tomatoes, water, red wine vinegar, thyme, tomato paste, and salt and pepper, stirring the mixture until combined. When brought to a boil, drop the heat as low as possible and let it simmer half an hour with the lid covering the pan. Remove the lid and let the rest of the water evaporate, stirring the mixture from time to time. Remove from heat, stir in balsamic vinegar, and let it to cool for 30 minutes. Serve cool.

Tip: Can be stored in a fridge less than 2 weeks.

Vegan Sushi

Preparation time: 40 minutes

Ingredients for 4 portions:

4-5 nori sheets
2 oz. ginger, ground
1 cup quinoa, prewashed and rinsed
2 cup water
1 avocado, sliced in stripes
1 medium cucumber, cut in long strips
1/2 cup baby carrots, cut in long strips

1 cup baby romaine lettuce
1tbsp. maple syrup or agave nectar, to liking
Tamari soy sauce, to taste
salt and pepper, to taste

Directions:

Cook quinoa, mixed with ginger until soft (about 15 minutes after boiling on medium heat). When done, remove from heat and stir in the maple syrup or the agave nectar with vinegar. Allow quinoa mixture to cool while you place a nori sheet on your bamboo mat.

Place the quinoa in the center of the nori sheet. Wet your fingertips (keep a bowl of cool water nearby) and spread the quinoa towards the edges of the sheet in a thin layer, leaving about an inch of sheet remaining on the edge farthest from you. Place a row of baby romaine leaves an inch or two from the closest edge. Top with a thin row of cucumber, carrot, and avocado slices. Roll the sushi roll using your bamboo mat. Set the roll aside and prepare the remaining ingredients the same way as above. Slice the rolls into cut-sized pieces and serve them with low sodium tamari soy sauce.

Quinoa with Seaweed

Preparation time: 40 minutes

Ingredients for 4 portions:

1 cup kombu seaweed,
1 cup quinoa
2 cups lukewarm water
1/4 cup white sesame seeds
2-3 tbsp. vinegar
1/2 tbsp. maple syrup or agave nectar
No salt, as kombu seaweed is a salt-alternative

Directions:
Bring to a boil a cup of quinoa with 2 cups of water. When boiling, remove from heat and let simmer until the water is absorbed. Place the kombu leaves into a bowl with the water. Let it hydrate, then remove from the water and chop. When quinoa is cool, mix with the seaweed and vinegar, sprinkling with as much nectar or syrup as you wish.
Tip: Add other fresh chopped vegetables and enjoy this healthy recipe various ways.

Dips:

Classic Hummus

Preparation time: 10 minutes

Ingredients for 4 portions:

3 cloves garlic, minced
1 can chickpeas, drained and rinsed
1 tsp Kosher salt
1/4 cup Tahini
1/4 cup lemon juice, to taste
1 tbsp. olive oil, more for drizzling on top
paprika for garnish

Directions:
Add the garlic, chickpeas, Kosher salt, tahini, lemon juice and
1 tablespoon of olive oil to your food processor. Process until
it is well combined and has a thick creamy texture. If it is too
thick, you can thin with additional lemon juice or additional
olive oil. Put into a bowl, and with a spoon make some valleys

37

or rivers on top for the added olive oil. Garnish with paprika if you like.

Beetroot Hummus

Preparation time: 10 minutes

Ingredients for 4 portions:

1/2 pound beets (about 4 medium sized beets)
2 tbsp. tahini sesame seed paste
5 tbsp. lemon juice
1 small clove garlic, chopped
1 tbsp. ground cumin
1 tbsp. lemon zest (zest from approx. 2 lemons)
generous pinch of sea salt or Kosher salt
pepper to taste, freshly ground

Directions:

To cook the beets, cut off any tops, scrub the roots clean, and put them in a covered dish with about 1/4-inch of water in a 375°F/190°C oven. Cook until easily penetrated with a knife or fork. Alternatively, cover with water in a saucepan and simmer until tender, about 1/2 hour. Peel once they have cooled.

Place all ingredients in a food processor (or blender) and pulse until smooth. Taste and adjust seasonings and ingredients as desired. Chill and store in the refrigerator for up to 3 days or freeze for longer storage. Eat with pita chips or with sliced cucumber or celery.

Avocado Dip

Preparation time: 5 minutes

Ingredients for 4 portions:

2 ripe avocados, pitted
2 cloves garlic, minced

1 lime, juiced
Kosher salt
black pepper, freshly ground

Directions:

Mash avocados in a large bowl. Add garlic and lime juice to the bowl. Serve seasoned with salt and pepper.

Roasted Pepper Dip

Preparation time: 15 minutes

Ingredients for 4 portions:

2 medium red bell peppers
1 tbsp. garlic, minced
1 tsp. extra-virgin olive oil
1 tbsp. balsamic vinegar
1 cup Vegan Sour Cream (please find our version of this cheese in the Vegan Cheese Recipes section of this book)
1 tbsp. basil, finely chopped
salt and pepper, freshly ground

Directions:

Roast the peppers over a gas flame or under the broiler until charred all over. Transfer to a bowl, cover with plastic wrap, and let steam for 20 minutes. Discard the skins, cores and seeds. Pat the peppers dry and finely chop them. In a skillet, cook the garlic in the oil over moderate heat until fragrant, about 30 seconds. Add the peppers and vinegar and cook over moderately low heat, stirring, until dry, about 12 minutes. Transfer to a bowl to cool. Stir in the Vegan Sour Cream and basil and season with salt and pepper. Refrigerate until chilled.

Tip: You will enjoy it cooked with or without sour cream.

Pesto Sauce

Preparation time: 40 minutes

Ingredients for 4 portions:

2 cups baby spinach leaves
1 cup basil leaves
5 gloves garlic, cut into large pieces
1/3 cup pine nuts
1/2 tsp. red pepper, crushed, to taste
1 lemon, juiced
1/2 cup olive oil
salt and pepper, to taste

Directions:

Blend all the ingredients with several tablespoons of the olive oil in a food-processor until almost smooth. Scrape the sides of the bowl when necessary. Sprinkle the remaining olive oil into the mixture gradually while processing. When smooth, can be served immediately. Should be kept in a fridge not more than a week.

Soups:

Tomatoe Soup

Preparation time: 15 minutes

Ingredients for 4 portions

For the soup:

1 tbsp. olive oil
1 medium yellow onion, medium diced
Kosher salt
2 medium garlic cloves, minced
Pinch of red pepper flakes (optional)
1 28-oz. can whole peeled tomatoes, preferably San Marzano's
1½ cups low-sodium chicken broth or water
black pepper, to taste, freshly ground

Optional garnishes (alone or in combination):

Extra-virgin olive oil
4 fresh basil leaves, julienned
Vegan Parmesan cheese, freshly grated (please find our version of this cheese in the Vegan Cheese Recipes section of this book)

Directions:

Place a medium saucepan over medium-low heat and add the oil. Add the onion and a big pinch of salt. Cook, stirring occasionally, until the onion is completely soft, about 15 minutes. If at any point the onion looks like it's beginning to brown, reduce the heat. Add the garlic and optional red pepper flakes and cook for 5 minutes more, stirring occasionally.

Increase the heat to medium and add the tomatoes and their juices to the pan. Roughly crush the tomatoes with the back of a wooden spoon and cook until they begin to soften, about 10 minutes. Add the broth or water and bring to a simmer. Cook at a medium simmer until the tomatoes begin to fall apart, about 15 minutes.

Remove the soup from the heat and cool slightly, about 10 minutes. Purée the soup directly in the saucepan using an immersion blender, or use a countertop blender, carefully puréeing the soup in a couple of batches until smooth.

Return the soup to the burner over low heat. Add black pepper, then taste and adjust the seasoning with additional salt or pepper as needed. Serve in warmed bowls as is or topped with the garnishes of your choice.

Lentil & Tomato Soup

Preparation time: 20 minutes

Ingredients for 4 portions:

1 tbsp. olive or vegetable oil
1 large onion, finely chopped (1 cup)
1 medium stalk celery, cut into ½-inch pieces
2 cloves garlic, finely chopped
2 medium carrots, cut into ½-inch pieces (1 cup)
1 cup (8 oz.) lentils dried, sorted, rinsed
4 cups water
4 tsp. vegetable bouillon granules
1 tsp. thyme leaves, dried
1/4 tsp. pepper
1 bay leaf, dried
1 can (28 oz.) Muir Glen™ organic diced tomatoes, undrained

Directions:

Heat oil in a 3-quart saucepan, over medium-high heat. Add onion, celery and garlic. Cook about 5 minutes, stirring occasionally, until softened. Stir in remaining ingredients except tomatoes. Heat to boiling. Reduce heat; cover and simmer 15 to 20 minutes or until lentils and vegetables are tender. Stir in tomatoes. Reduce heat and simmer uncovered about 15 minutes or until thoroughly heated. Remove bay leaf.

Mushroom Soup

Preparation time: 10 minutes

Ingredients for 4 portions:

1 large white onion, diced
1 package (10 oz.) white button mushrooms, sliced
1 package (10 oz.) baby Portobello mushrooms, sliced
10 stalks thyme, fresh, leaves removed
1 cup organic vegetable broth
1 tbsp. tapioca flour

1 cup almond or cashew milk (unsweetened)
1 dried bay leaf
1/2 tbsp. liquid aminos (GF) (or soy sauce)
1/2 tsp. salt
black pepper, freshly ground

Directions:

Add the diced onions to a large saucepan over medium heat. Allow onions to sweat while slicing the mushrooms, about 5-7 minutes. Move onions to the sides of the saucepan and add mushrooms, allow to cook 5 minutes uncovered. Stir the onions and mushrooms together. Add fresh thyme and continue to cook at least 10 minutes. You will notice a substantial amount of water has come out of the mushrooms, and they are reduced in volume by half. Add the bay leaf, the salt and the liquid aminos to the mushrooms. Stir tapioca flour into the organic broth. Add to mushrooms and stir. Add almond milk. Allow to cook for at least 15 minutes, stirring occasionally. Taste and add freshly ground black pepper to taste.

Tip: This soup is amazing the next day as well and can easily be doubled. Add cashew cheese, Vegan Parmesan cheese, or enjoy the soup just as it is!

Pumpkin Soup

Preparation time: 20 minutes

Ingredients for 4 portions:

2 lb. pumpkin (any), chopped into large chunks (remove skin and seeds)
2 medium onions, sliced
2 cloves of garlic
3 cups vegetable stock
1 cup milk (see notes for Vegan subs)
salt and pepper

Directions:
Combine all ingredients except salt and pepper in a saucepan and bring to a boil. Reduce heat and let simmer until pumpkin is tender. Remove from heat and use a stick blender to blend until smooth. If you don't have a stick blender, use a regular. Season to taste with salt and pepper, then serve with crusty bread.

Tip: For a richer finish, substitute the Vegan milk with Vegan sour cream, but add after blending and do not bring to a boil.

Carrot Soup

Preparation time: 40 minutes

Ingredients for 4 portions:

4 large carrots, sliced
5 new potatoes, quartered
1 large onion, diced
3 cloves garlic, minced
2 cups vegetable broth
2 tbsp. ginger, fresh, grated
1 tbsp. curry powder
1 tbsp. olive oil
salt and pepper, to taste

Directions:
Place onion, garlic, and oil in a pan and cook, stirring until onions are transparent. Add carrots and potatoes and allow the carrots to evaporate the juices. Pour the broth into a pot with the vegetables and add ginger, curry powder, salt and

pepper. Bring the soup to a boil, then reduce heat to low. Simmer for 20 minutes, until vegetables are soft. Put the vegetables into a food-processor and combine thoroughly. When the pureed soup is ready, reheat it once again and serve!

Minestrone Soup

Preparation time: 25 minutes

Ingredients for 4 portions:

1 tbsp. olive oil
1 medium brown onion, finely chopped
1 celery stalk, trimmed, finely chopped
1 large carrot, peeled, chopped
2 garlic cloves, crushed
4 cups Massel vegetable liquid stock
2 tbsp. tomato paste
3 large ripe tomatoes, chopped
3/4 cup Vetta small shell dried pasta
12 oz. can Cannellini beans, drained, rinsed

2 small zucchini, chopped
1/2 cup peas, frozen
1/2 cup roughly chopped fresh basil leaves
Vegan Parmesan cheese, to serve, finely grated (please find
our version of this cheese in Vegan Cheese Recipes section
of this book)

Directions:

Heat oil in a large saucepan over high heat. onion, celery,
carrots and garlic. Cook, stirring, for 3 to 4 minutes or until
onion has softened.
Add stock, tomato paste, tomato, and 1 cup cold water. Bring
to a boil. Reduce heat to low. Simmer, covered, for 30 minutes
or until vegetables are tender. Add pasta, beans, zucchini and
peas. Simmer for 15 minutes or until pasta is tender. Stir in
basil. Top with Vegan cheese. Serve.

Miso Soup

Preparation time: 40 minutes

Ingredients for 4 portions:

1/4 cup dark miso
4 mushrooms, dried or any mushrooms to your liking, fresh
1/2 cup firm Tofu cheese, to liking, diced
1 cup boiling water
1/4 cup cold water
7 cups hot vegetable broth
1 bunch green onions or lettuce, chopped
2 carrots, grated
2 cloves garlic, minced
1 tbsp. ginger, fresh and minced
2 tbsp. sesame seeds oil
1/4 cup rice wine vinegar
3 tbsp. tamari soy sauce
pinch of cayenne pepper

Directions:

Note: If you use dried mushrooms, place them in a bowl with boiling water and keep covered with a lid for 10 minutes. If you use fresh mushrooms, bring them to a boil and keep the broth apart.

Simmer the lettuce/onions, garlic, and ginger in a vegetable broth for 5 minutes. Add the Vegan Tofu and simmer several minutes more. Add vinegar, tamari sauce, cayenne and sesame oil. Stir either the soaking liquid or the mushroom broth into the soup. Slice the mushrooms and add them. Place the miso into a cup and mash in 1/2 cup of the soup until smooth. Add the miso mixed liquid to the soup, then add the carrots. Heat it until it begins to boil. Taste and add seasoning as needed. Serve immediately.

Noodles soup

Preparation time: 40 minutes

Ingredients for 4 portions:

1 cup uncooked rice noodles
1 carrot, finely sliced
2 bell peppers, sliced
1/2 cup green onion, chopped
2 cloves garlic, minced
1 tsp. ginger, fresh and minced
1/2 cup celery
3 cups vegetable stock
1/8 cup soy sauce – gluten free
3 tbsp. olive oil
1 pinch of thyme, fresh
1 bay leaf

Directions:

Pour some olive oil into the pot and let it heat. Add the veggies and sauté until soft but not brown. Add the broth and bring to a boil. Last add the noodles and cook until ready, not more than 10 minutes. Serve hot.

Hot dishes:

Baked Spicy Potatoes

Preparation time: 30 minutes

Ingredients for 4 portions:

2½ pounds potatoes (or 3 pounds for less spicy potatoes)
2 tbsp. olive oil
2 garlic cloves, minced (or maybe 1/2 tsp. garlic powder)
2 tsp. parsley, dried
1/2 tsp. cayenne
1/2 tsp. paprika
3/4 tsp. salt
1/2 tsp. pepper

Directions:
Preheat the oven to 450°F/230°C. Pour the olive oil onto a
rimmed cookie sheet. Add the spices and mix with the olive

oil. Clean the potatoes and slice the potato into even wedges. Put the potatoes on the cookie sheet and use your hands to coat the potatoes with the olive oil mix. The baking time will vary depending on how big your wedges are. I usually bake mine for 20 minutes, take them out of the oven to flip them, and bake for another 10 – 15 minutes. If you want them crispier, just bake them for a few minutes longer.

Baked Sweet Potatoes

Preparation time: 5 minutes

Ingredients for 4 portions:

4 medium sweet potatoes, scrubbed

Directions:

Preheat the oven to 425ºF/220ºC. Scrub sweet potatoes and pierce in several places with a sharp knife. Line a baking sheet with foil and place the potatoes on top. Bake for 45 minutes to an hour, depending on the size of the potatoes, until thoroughly soft and beginning to ooze. Remove from the heat. Place on a plate or in a dish and allow to cool. Cover with plastic wrap and refrigerate (they will continue to ooze and sweeten). Serve cold (cut and remove the skin) or at room temperature, or reheat for 20 to 30 minutes in a 350°F/175°C oven.

Fried Vegetables

Preparation time: 15 minutes

Ingredients for 4 portions:

1 tbsp. olive oil
1 medium onion, sliced thin
1 cup carrots, diagonally sliced
2 cups broccoli florets
2 cups sugar snap peas
1 large red bell pepper, cut into strips
1 tbsp. reduced sodium soy sauce
1 tsp. garlic powder
1 tsp. ginger, ground

2 tsp. sesame seed, toasted
salt and pepper, to taste

Directions:

Heat the oil in a wok or large deep skillet on medium-high heat. Add onion and carrots; stir fry 2 minutes. Add remaining vegetables; stir fry 5 to 7 minutes or until vegetables are tender-crisp. Add soy sauce, garlic powder and ginger; stir-fry until well blended. Sprinkle with sesame seeds. Serve over cooked rice, if desired.

Curried Couscous with Vegetables

Preparation time: 15 minutes

Ingredients for 4 portions:

1 large onion, cut in thin wedges
2 cups yellow summer squash and/or zucchini (2 medium), coarsely chopped

2½-oz. cans tomatoes with jalapeno peppers, diced
2 cups water
2 5.7-oz. packages curry-flavor couscous mix
1 cup almonds, chopped toasted slivered
1/2 cup raisins (optional)
cilantro sprigs (optional)
salt and pepper, to taste

Directions:

In a 3½- or 4-quart slow cooker, combine onion, summer squash, undrained tomatoes, water, and seasoning packets from couscous mixes. Cover and cook on low heat setting for 4 to 6 hours or on high heat setting for 2 to 3 hours. Stir in couscous. Turn off cooker. Cover and let stand for 5 minutes. Fluff couscous mixture with a fork. To serve, sprinkle each serving with almonds and raisins. If desired, garnish with cilantro sprigs.

Grilled Vegetables

Preparation time: 10 minutes

Ingredients for 4 portions:

1 lb. cremini mushrooms, cleaned
2 cups cauliflower, cut into small florets
2 cups cocktail tomatoes
12 cloves garlic, minced
2 tbsp. olive oil
salt and pepper to taste
1 tbsp. fresh parsley, chopped
1 tsp. fresh Italian parsley leaves, chopped
1 tsp. basil leaves, chopped fresh
1/2 tsp. fresh rosemary leaves, finely chopped

Directions:

Preheat oven to 400 F. In a bowl add all the mushrooms and veggies. Drizzle with olive oil then add fresh Italian parsley leaves, fresh basil leaves, fresh rosemary leaves, salt, and pepper; toss until well combined. Dump the veggies onto a baking sheet and place in the preheated oven. Roast for 20 to 30 minutes or until mushrooms are golden brown and cauliflower is fork-tender. Garnish with fresh parsley before serving.

Stewed Beans in Tomato Sauce

Preparation time: 10 minutes

Ingredients for 4 portions:

1 lb. dried white beans, such as Great Northern or cannellini, picked over, rinsed, and drained
1 onion, 1 half finely chopped (1/2 cup)
1 carrot, cut crosswise into thirds
1 celery stalk, cut crosswise into thirds
1 dried bay leaf
1 can (28 oz.) whole plum tomatoes, with juice
2 tbsp. extra-virgin olive oil, plus more for drizzling
2 garlic cloves, minced
1/8 tsp. red-pepper flakes
1 sprig rosemary
coarse salt and pepper, freshly ground

Directions:

Soak beans in water overnight. Drain, and transfer to a large pot. Cover beans with 4 inches water. Add the intact half of the onion, the carrot, celery, and bay leaf. Bring to a boil. Reduce heat, and simmer until beans are tender but not bursting, about 1 hour. Drain, and remove onion, carrot, celery, and bay leaf; discard. Pulse tomatoes, with juice, in a food processor until coarsely chopped. Heat oil in a medium heavy-bottomed pot over medium heat. Add chopped onion, garlic, and red-pepper flakes. Cook, stirring occasionally, until onion and garlic are tender but not browned, about 3 minutes. Add tomatoes and rosemary. Bring to a boil. Add beans and simmer, stirring occasionally, until tomato sauce thickens (about 20 minutes). Season with salt and pepper. Serve warm, and drizzle with oil just before serving.

Biryani Rice

Preparation time: 25 minutes

Ingredients for 4 portions:

2 cups basmati rice
3 cloves garlic crushed in a garlic press
1 tsp. ground cumin
1/2 tsp. ground turmeric
1/4 tsp. cayenne pepper or to taste
3 tbsp. olive or canola oil
4 tsp. lemon juice
1/4 cup fresh cilantro or parsley, chopped
4 cardamom pods
2⅔ cups vegetable stock
salt and black pepper, freshly ground

Directions:

Wash the rice in several changes of water and drain. Cover
generously with fresh water and leave to soak for 30 minutes.
Drain. Pour oil into a heavy, medium pan and set over
medium-high heat. Put the cardamom pods in the pan and
sauté for about 10-15 seconds. Add the garlic and sauté for
another 10 seconds. Add the vegetable stock, bring to a boil.
Add the lemon juice, cumin, turmeric, cayenne, black pepper
and salt
Add the drained rice and bring to a boil again. Cover tightly,
turn heat to very, very low, and cook for about 25 minutes or
until rice is soft. Turn off the heat. Stir gently to mix and keep
covered until needed.

Vegan Paella

Preparation time: 20 minutes

Ingredients for 4 portions:

2½ cups vegetable stock
1/2 tsp. Saffron threads
1 1/2 tbsp. olive oil
1 large red onion, sliced
1 yellow bell pepper, sliced
1 red bell pepper, sliced
1 cup brown mushrooms, sliced
3 cloves garlic, minced
1 cup Bomba rice
2 roma tomatoes, chopped
1½ tsp. paprika, smoked
1 cup green peas
1 can artichoke hearts, drained and chopped
1/2 cup parsley, chopped
salt and pepper, freshly ground, to taste

Directions:

Combine the stock and saffron threads in a medium saucepan and bring to a boil over high heat. Reduce heat to low and maintain a simmer. Meanwhile, heat paella pan on the stove with 1½ tablespoons olive oil. Add onion to paella pan and sauté for 2 minutes. Add sliced red and yellow pepper and continue to sauté until softened, about 5 minutes. Add the mushrooms and garlic and sauté for 5 minutes or until it has softened slightly. Season liberally with salt and pepper. Increase heat to medium-high. Add Bomba rice, tomato and smoked paprika and cook, stirring, for 1 minute until well mixed through. Reduce heat to medium-low. Add one-third of the saffron infused stock and stir until just combined. Let simmer uncovered for 5 minutes or until liquid is almost absorbed. Add the next third of the stock and cook for 5 minutes uncovered or until almost absorbed. Add remaining third of stock and cook for 5-10 minutes uncovered.
Sprinkle surface of paella with peas and artichoke hearts. Cover entire pan in tin foil and leave to cook on a low heat for 12 minutes. After 12 minutes, turn heat off but leave the paella pan covered with tin foil for another 10 minutes. Remove tin foil after 10 minutes and garnish with parsley.

Rice with Fresh Vegetables

Preparation time: 20 minutes

Ingredients for 4 portions:

1/2 cup orzo pasta or broken spaghetti
1 tbsp. extra-virgin olive oil
1 bunch asparagus, trimmed and chopped into 1-inch pieces
on an angle
1 carrot, cut into short matchsticks
2 shallots, chopped
2 cloves garlic, chopped
2½ cups chicken or vegetable stock
1 cup long-grain white rice
1 tbsp. lemon zest, plus the juice of 1/2 lemon
1 tbsp. fresh thyme, chopped
1 bunch arugula, chopped
about 1 cup Vegan Almond Cheese, grated (please find our
version of this cheese in the Vegan Cheese Recipes section
of this book)
salt and pepper, freshly ground

Directions:

Preheat a medium pot over medium-high heat. Add the pasta and cook until nutty and deep golden brown. Add the extra-virgin olive oil, make 1 turn of the pan, then add the asparagus, carrot, shallots, and garlic; season with salt and pepper. Cover and cook to sweat the vegetables a bit, stirring occasionally, for 5 minutes. Stir in the stock, rice, lemon zest, thyme and browned pasta and bring to a boil. Cover the pot, lower the heat, and simmer until the rice is just tender, 16 to 18 minutes. Fold in the arugula, then stir in the lemon juice and Vegan cheese.

Eggplant Pasta

Preparation time: 15 minutes

Ingredients for 4 portions:

1 pound large eggplant
1 tbsp. olive oil
1/4 tsp. garlic, minced
1/4 tsp. red pepper flakes

1 small tomato, seeded and chopped
3 tbsp. Vegan sour cream (easy recipe here)
1 tbsp. basil, chiffonade
2 tbsp. Vegan Parmesan cheese, grated (please find our
version of this cheese in the Vegan Cheese Recipes section
of this book)
1 tbsp. breadcrumbs
¼ cup pomegranate seeds
kosher salt

Directions:

Peel the eggplant, leaving 1 inch of skin at the top and bottom.
Slice the eggplant lengthwise into 1/4-inch-thick slices (I would
use a mandolin for this). Place the eggplant slices on a cooling
rack set over the sink and generously sprinkle with kosher
salt. Wait 15 minutes, flip, sprinkle again, and wait another 15
minutes. Rinse thoroughly under cool water and gently
squeeze out excess water. Place on paper towels and pat dry,
then cut the slices into 1/4-inch-wide strips so that they
resemble linguine. Heat a 10-inch sauté pan over medium-
high heat and add the oil. When it shimmers, add the garlic
and red pepper flakes and toss for 10 seconds. Add the
eggplant and toss to coat. Add the tomato and toss for 15 to
20 seconds. Add the fresh Vegan sour cream and toss for
another 10 seconds. Finish with the basil and Vegan
Parmesan. Transfer to a serving dish, top with breadcrumbs,
sprinkle the pomegranate seeds, toss, and serve immediately.

Stuffed Mushrooms

Preparation time: 30 minutes

Ingredients for 4 portions:

8 small/medium size Portobello mushrooms
1 small stalk celery
2 cloves garlic, finely chopped
1/2 slice ginger, fresh
1 large onion, finely chopped
2 small red bell peppers, finely chopped
3 tbsp. pine nuts
4 tbsp. olive oil
2 tsp. soy sauce
salt and pepper and/or chili, to liking

Directions:

Cut and finely dice the stems of the mushrooms. Precook mushroom stems, ginger, garlic, and pepper in the olive oil. Stir in all other ingredients into the vegetable mix after it is removed from heat. Oil the mushrooms and put them on a baking pan. Stuff the mushrooms, mounding them with the mix generously. Cook in the oven for 15-20 minutes, until the top is crispy crust. Top the cooked mushrooms with some fresh herbs for a nice decor.

Fried Tomatoes

Preparation time: 40 minutes

Ingredients for 4 portions:

8 ripe plum tomatoes, halved
2 tbsp. basil leaves, freshly chopped
1 tbsp. oregano, dry
1 tbsp. basil, dry
2 tbsp. rosemary, sprigs
2 cloves garlic, minced
3 tbsp. olive oil
salt and pepper, to taste

Directions:

Add some olive oil to a frying pan, place tomatoes cut-sides up. Sprinkle them with all of the herbs and garlic and drizzle with some olive oil on top. Cover and cook on a lower heat for at least 5 minutes, then remove the cover and cook until browned underneath. Top with some fresh greenery and serve immediately.

Vegan Curry

Preparation time: 40 minutes

Ingredients for 4 portions:

2 pounds butternut squash, finely chopped
4 Portobello mushrooms, cut into 4 pieces each
1 large onion, diced
1 tbsp. garlic, minced
2 Granny Smith apples, diced
2 carrots, cut into chunks
1 tbsp. curry powder
1/4 tbsp. cinnamon powder

1 tsp. ginger, fresh and minced
2 bay leaves
3 cups vegetable stock broth
1/2 cup Vegan Sour Cream (please find our version of this cheese in the Vegan Cheese Recipes section of this book)
salt and black pepper, to taste

Directions:

Add all the ingredients to the vegetable broth. Allow it to cook on the low heat setting for 4-5 hours. The vegetables are done when you can easily pierce them with a knife. Stir in the Vegan Sour Cream and adjust the curry powder, salt, and pepper to your taste. Serve warm with saltine crackers.

Nut Cutlets

Preparation time: 40 minutes

Ingredients for 4 portions:

3 tbsp. all-purpose flour
2 cups breadcrumbs

2 cups potatoes, boiled and mashed
2 tbsp. nuts (peanuts or groundnuts)
2 tbsp. cashews
2 tbsp. almonds, blanched
1 slice of bread
2-3 chilies, green
1 tbsp. ginger, finely chopped
1/2 cup cilantro
1/4 lemon, juiced
oil for frying
1/2 cup water
salt and pepper, to taste

Directions:

Chop all the nuts with a chopper or with a knife to medium size. Thoroughly mix the mashed potatoes, flour, bread, nuts, cilantro, and chilies and add some salt to taste. In a separate bowl, mix the flour with the water to make a thin paste. Form the nut mixture into cutlets of a desired shape, dip them into the flour paste and coat with the breadcrumbs. Fry the cutlets in a pan on medium heat by tossing them gently. This way you can cook it with minimum oil. Serve warm or cool, as you prefer.

Veggie Balls

Preparation time: 40 minutes

Ingredients for 4 portions:

4-5 oz. frozen peas
1 large onion, finely chopped
1/2 cup sunflower or rapeseed oil for frying
1 red bell pepper, finely chopped
2 carrots, finely chopped
2-3 cloves garlic, minced
1 cup kale, chopped or minced
12-oz. tin of chickpeas
2 tbsp. olive oil
1 tbsp. vegetable stock powder
1/2 cup gram flour
flour for dusting
salt and pepper, to taste

Sauce:

1 tbsp. dairy-free margarine
7 oz. soya milk

1/2 cup boiling water
1tsp. vegetable stock powder
2 tbsp. mustard
1 tbsp. flour
soy sauce

Directions:

Drain and rinse the chickpeas. In a food-processor, blend with olive oil until smooth. Cook the peas in a microwave for 2 minutes and then drain. Cook the onion with garlic in a preheated saucepan over a medium heat for a minute. Add carrots to the onion, along with pepper, cooked peas and kale. Let cook over a medium heat. Add some stock powder, gram flour, and season thoroughly with salt and pepper. Mix all ingredients and remove from heat. Sprinkle your hands and a chopping board with a little flour. Roll the mixture into teaspoon-size balls and place them onto the board. You might have about 20 vegan "meatballs." Pour some oil into the frying pan with rapeseed or sunflower oil. Fry the meatballs, turning them until they are golden-brown all over. Remove from the frying pan and place on a plate with a kitchen towel/paper to drain the extra oil.

For the sauce: heat the margarine, stir through the flour, and cook on a low setting for a few minutes. Add the vegan milk and stock powder, adjust with the boiling water and cook, stirring until thick. Add the mustard and stir, then add a few drops of soy sauce to taste. Serve the meatballs with the sauce poured over the top, with any hot dish you prefer.

Korean Cabbage Kimchi in Chili Sauce

Preparation time: 7 hours

Ingredients for 4 portions:

1 Korean cabbage, 1/2 sliced and 1/2 whole
1½ warm cups of water
5-6 cloves garlic
1 tbsp. ginger, fresh
5-6 tbsp. Korean chili powder or 3 large red chilies, chopped
2 tbsp. soy sauce
3-4 green shallots, sliced
1/2 cup of herbs, celery or other, to taste
sea salt to taste

Directions:

Place cabbage in a large bowl. Sprinkle with salt. Pour over the water. Stir to combine thoroughly. Leave for an hour or so. Rinse the cabbage later and drain well. In a food-processor mix the garlic, ginger, and chili until finely chopped.

Add soy sauce and shallots to the garlic mixture and mix the cabbage. Combine with your hands and then keep in a closed bowl for at least 5 hours for fermenting. Can be stored in a fridge for several months.

Roasted Eggplant with Asparagus

Preparation time: 40 minutes
Preheated oven 400 degrees.

Ingredients for 4 portions:

1 bunch asparagus with trimmed bottoms
1 eggplant, sliced
olive oil to taste
3 cloves garlic, minced
1/2 lemon, juiced
any herbs to liking
salt and pepper, freshly ground, to taste

Directions:

Prepare the dressing beforehand: mix garlic, parsley and lemon juice well. Mix eggplant slices with some salt and pepper and let stand for half an hour, then blot dry. Oil them with the olive oil. Add more salt and pepper to taste, then toss with asparagus. Place eggplant slices and asparagus on a baking sheet and roast until soft. Serve with the dressing.

Pasta:

Farfalle with Pesto and Tomatoes

Preparation time: 30 minutes

Ingredients for 4 portions:

1 lb. Farfalle
2 cups cherry or regular tomatoes, halved or chopped into small pieces
6 oz. arugula (rucola),
1 clove garlic

1/4 cup fresh parsley leaves, chopped
1/4 cup any Vegan cheese, grated (please find our version of this cheese in the Vegan Cheese Recipes section of this book)
1/3 cup olive oil
salt and pepper, to taste

Directions:

For pesto, mix arugula, parsley, walnuts, and garlic in a blender until finely chopped. Add cheese, salt and pepper, and some olive oil until the sauce is smooth. Put the pasta into a pan of boiling of water – 1/4 of a pan. Stir gently until pasta is cooked and then drain it well. Place the pasta mixed with the pesto into a serving bowl. Toss well. Add tomatoes and toss again.

Tip: Use the pasta cooking water if you wish to thin the sauce.

Fusille with Cashews, Vegan Cheese and Dried Tomatoes

Preparation time: 30 minutes

Ingredients for 4 portions:

8 oz. Fusille pasta
1 cup of dried tomatoes, chopped
4 oz. Vegan Mozarella cheese, soft and fresh, cut into cubes
(please find our version of this cheese in the Vegan Cheese
Recipes section of this book)
1tbsp. thyme, fresh
4 cloves of garlic, minced
1 tbsp. olive oil
1/2 cup cashew nuts
Salt, pepper, and other herbs, to taste

Directions:

Cook pasta in a pan 3/4 full of boiling water until done, then
drain it. Prepare all ingredients as the water boils and pasta is
cooked. Add all ingredients: tomatoes, Vegan cheese,
cashews. Stir in garlic, salt, pepper and olive oil. Serve with
fresh leaves of thyme or basil.

Spaghetti with Mushrooms

Preparation time: 40 minutes

Ingredients for 4 portions:

1 lb. uncooked spaghetti
1pound Cremini mushrooms, sliced
4 tbsp. olive oil
5 cloves garlic, minced
1 cup Vegan Zucchini cheese, grated (please find our version of this cheese in the Vegan Cheese recipes section of this book)
1 pinch of parsley, fresh and chopped
water
salt and pepper to taste

Directions:

Cook pasta in a pan 3/4 full of boiling water until done, then drain it. Reserve 3/4 cup of pasta cooking water. Oil a pan, add the mushrooms, season with salt and pepper, and sauté about 5 minutes until browned.

Add garlic and remains of olive oil and sauté 2 minutes more. Add the spaghetti, adjust the cooking water and grated cheese. Toss gently and stir until the water has just evaporated, not more than 2 minutes. Add the parsley and toss again to combine. Serve in bowls. Top with some cheese.

Cauliflower Pasta

Preparation time: 40 minutes

Ingredients for 4 portions:

1 small head cauliflower, stems removed, florets separated
3 tbsp. olive oil
3 cloves garlic, minced
salt, pepper, and red pepper flakes, to taste
2 cups vegetable broth for flavor
2 oz. spaghetti, fettuccini
parsley, fresh, chopped
1/2 cup Vegan Parmesan cheese, grated (please find our version of this cheese in the Vegan Cheese Recipes section of this book)

Directions:

Add cauliflower to a bowl with olive oil, garlic, red pepper flakes and salt. Toss gently. Place the mixture onto a baking sheet and roast for 20 minutes. As it is being prepared, add 2 cups vegetable broth to a pan with 5 cups water and bring to a boil. Add the pasta and cook as per instructions for not more than 10 minutes, Drain and set aside. Add cooked pasta, parsley, minced garlic, Vegan Parmesan cheese, and cauliflower. Toss to coat. Remove from heat and sample. Adjust seasoning with salt and pepper and parsley as desired. Serve hot, adding the cheese on top of each serving.

Pasta Salad

Preparation time: 40 minutes

Ingredients for 4 portions:

12 oz. pasta
15 oz. (1 can) chickpeas, drained
1 small bell pepper, yellow, chopped
1½ cups cherry tomatoes, halved

1½ cups cucumber, fresh, chopped
1/2 cup canned corn
1/2 cup olives, halved
1 small onion, finely sliced
3 tbsp. dill, chopped
red pepper flakes, salt, and pepper, to taste

Dressing:

1/3 cup of water
1 lemon, juiced
3 cloves garlic, minced
olive oil, to liking
salt to liking

Directions:

Cook pasta in a pan 3/4 full of boiling water until done, then drain it. Add all ingredients into a bowl and mix until combined. Add pasta to the vegetables. Mix well and season with salt to taste. Can be served either warm or chilled.

Dumplings with Spinach and Mushrooms

Preparation time: 40 minutes

Ingredients for 4 portions:

1 lb. Basic Dumpling Dough
4 cups or 8 oz. spinach, chopped coarsely
4 large shiitake mushrooms, stemmed and chopped, soaked
(liquid reserved)
1/3 cup carrot, finely chopped
3 oz. Tofu Cheese, brown, pressed, finely chopped
1½ tbsp. soy sauce
1 tbsp. ginger, freshly minced
2 tbsp. sesame oil
2/3 cup soy sauce
cornstarch for thickening the filling
salt and white pepper, to taste

Basic Dumpling Dough:

1½ cup water
1 cup all-purpose flour
1/2 tbsp. salt

Directions:

For the spinach: Cover the spinach with boiling water in a
bowl. Let it wilt for 30 seconds, drain and rinse with cold water,
drain again. Finally, the spinach can be packed into a cup.

For the flavoring sauce and filling: Combine the mushroom
water with salt and white pepper, soy sauce and sesame oil.
Set aside. In a frying pan, oil the ginger and stir it 30 seconds
until it releases its aroma. Add spinach, carrot, mushrooms,
and pressed Tofu and stir to combine. Pour the flavoring
sauce onto the mixture, stir until combined, and add starch
until it is thickened. Let it cool until room temperature. There
should be about 2 cups of filling.

For the dumpling dough: Mix together flour, water and salt. Knead until not sticky. Let it rest.

Form 16 wrappers from the dough. Each should be 3¼ inch in diameter. To assemble the dumplings, hold a wrapper in a cupped hand. Place a tablespoon of filling and position it slightly off-center toward the upper half of the wrapper, pressing and shaping it into a flat form. Fold, pleat and press to create a half-moon or otherwise-shaped dumpling. While you are making the remaining dumplings, keep the finished ones covered with a towel. If you will steam the dumplings right away, place the finished dumplings in a steamer tray, sealed side up. To cook, steam the dumplings over boiling water for about 8 minutes, until slightly transparent. Serve immediately with the sauce.
The remaining dumplings, if not steamed this time, can be covered with plastic wrap and refrigerated.

Pizza:

The following *Vegan Mozzarella Cheese* is used in cooking most of the pizza recipes.

Vegan Mozzarella Ingredients:

1/2 cup raw cashews, soaked in hot water for 30 minutes
1 cup hot water
3 tbsp. tapioca starch
1 tbsp. nutritional yeast
1 tsp. apple cider vinegar
1/2 tsp. salt
1/4 tsp. onion powder
1/4 tsp. garlic powder
1/8 tsp. white pepper

Directions:

Drain and rinse the cashews and place them in a blender with the rest of the ingredients. Blend until smooth. Transfer to a saucepan, stirring the cheese constantly. 1-2 min. later, cheese will start to get thick. Keep stirring until the cheese begins to move together while stirring. Remove from heat and let cool while preparing the other ingredients.

Pizza Margarita

Preparation time: 35 minutes

Ingredients for 4 portions:

Vegan Mozzarella cheese

Pizza Dough:

1 Roma tomato, thinly sliced
1 handful of fresh basil, chopped
red pepper flakes, optional

Sauce:

1 tbsp. olive oil
1 small white onion, minced
3-4 cloves garlic, minced
1 cup crushed tomatoes
2 tbsp. tomato paste
2 tsp. sugar
1/2 tsp. dried basil
1/2 tsp. dried oregano
1/2 tsp. dried thyme
salt and pepper, to taste

Directions

Heat the oil in a small saucepan. Add onion and garlic and sauté for 4-5 minutes. Stir in the remaining sauce ingredients and bring to a simmer. Meanwhile, brush the pizza base, rolled in circle or any other shape, with olive oil. Top it with tomato sauce, roma tomatoes, and spoonfuls of mozzarella. Bake for about 10 minutes in a 390°F/200°C oven. The pizza is done when the edges are crisp and light-brown. Remove from oven, top with basil and red pepper flakes, and serve immediately.

Pizza with Pesto, Rucola, and Dried Tomatoes

Preparation time: 45 minutes

Ingredients for 4 portions:

11 oz. pizza dough base, rolled thin
3 cups fresh rucola leaves
1/2 cup pesto
1/3 cup dried tomatoes

1 black pepper, freshly ground
1/2 cup olive oil, extra virgin
1/2 cup Vegan Mozzarella cheese, grated, for topping
salt and pepper, to taste

Directions:

Cover a baking tray with parchment paper to prevent sticking.
Sprinkle bottom of pizza base with olive oil and place it on the
tray. Bake the crust in a preheated to 390°F/200°C oven for
several minutes. Remove from heat and set aside. Apply
pesto to pizza crust. Sprinkle with dried tomatoes and crumble
the Vegan Mozzarella cheese and pepper on top. Bake for 10
minutes more until the crust is light brown. Remove from heat
and top with some rucola leaves.

Pizza with Mushrooms and Corn

Preparation time: 45 minutes

Ingredients for 2-3 portions:

11-oz. pizza base, rolled thin
1/2 cup Vegan zucchini cheese (please find our version of this cheese in the Vegan Cheese Recipes section of this book)
3-4 tbsp. Vegan Parmesan cheese, minced (please find our version of this cheese in the Vegan Cheese recipes section of this book)
2-3 tbsp. Vegan Mozzarella cheese, spread
2 cups tomato pizza sauce
1 onion, sliced
1 cup canned sweet corn
5-6 Portobello or white mushrooms, boiled and sliced
1 large tomato, sliced
3 tbsp. olive oil
oregano and other herbs to taste, dry
salt and pepper, to taste

Directions:

Cover a baking tray with parchment paper to prevent sticking. Place pizza base on it. Spread the tomato pizza sauce onto the pizza base. Spread the Vegan Mozzarella cheese with a knife all over the crust. Add Vegan Parmesan and Vegan Zucchini cheese all over, generously. Place mushrooms, oregano, onion, and corn on the pizza base. Top with some cheese and oregano again. Drizzle some olive oil. Bake for 10-15 minutes in a preheated to390°F/200°C oven until the base becomes golden brown. Serve warm.

Tip: Please visit our Vegan Cheese section for a good alternative for any of the vegan cheeses used in this recipe.

Pizza with Zucchini and Spinach

Preparation time: 45 minutes

Ingredients for 1 pizza (2-3 portions):

11-oz. pizza base, rolled thin
1 cup tomato pizza sauce
1 medium zucchini, sliced
1 red bell pepper, finely chopped
1 cup raw spinach, chopped
1 onion, finely chopped
1 cup any Vegan cheese, grated, (please check the Vegan
Cheese Recipes section of this book)
1 cup Vegan Mozzarella, grated
salt and pepper, to taste

Directions:

Cover a baking tray with parchment paper to prevent sticking.
Apply tomato sauce generously and add Vegan Mozzarella
cheese, onion, pepper, spinach, zucchini, and tomatoes onto
the pizza base. Add some Vegan minced cheese on top.
Place pizza in the oven and bake in a preheated to
390°F/200°C oven until it is golden brown. Remove from oven
and serve warm.

Pizza with Olives, Peppers, and Mushrooms

Preparation time: 45 minutes

Ingredients for 1 pizza (2-3 portions):

11-oz. pizza base, rolled thin
1/2 cup tomato pizza sauce
1 cup Vegan Almond cheese, grated
1/2 cup of black olives, sliced
1 green bell pepper, cut into strips
1 onion, finely chopped

2 cloves garlic, minced
1/4 tsp. dried oregano and other herbs
3 tbsp. olive oil
salt and pepper, to taste

Directions:

Cover the baking tray with parchment paper to prevent
sticking. Place pizza base rolled in a circle (or any other form)
on the tray. Spread tomato pizza sauce onto the base and
sprinkle some herbs over it. Sprinkle some salt and olive oil
over the mushrooms and put them on the grill for a couple of
minutes. Apply Vegan Almond cheese (or other Vegan cheese
to your liking), mushrooms, peppers, olives, and green
peppers on top. Add some more oregano and put the pizza
into preheated to 390°F/200°C oven. After 15 minutes, remove
and serve hot.

Pizza with Eggplants

Preparation time: 40 minutes

Ingredients for 4 portions:

11-oz. pizza base, rolled thin
1/2 cup tomato pizza sauce
1 medium sized eggplant, finely sliced
1/2 onion, finely sliced
2 cloves garlic, minced
1/2 cup Vegan Mozzarella cheese, grated
2 tbsp. rosemary, fresh, finely chopped
4 tbsp. olive oil
salt and pepper, to taste

Directions:

Cover a baking tray with parchment paper to prevent sticking. Place pizza base rolled in a circle (or any other form) on the tray. Spread tomato pizza sauce onto the base, and sprinkle some herbs and grated Vegan Mozzarella over it. Heat 1 tbsp. olive oil in a pan and sauté onions until caramelized-dark and fragrant-not more than 10 minutes. Add garlic and sauté for a minute more. Remove from heat. Place the eggplant slices on your pizza crust, covering the crust surface allover. Top with onions and add fresh rosemary on top. Bake in a preheated to 390°F/200°C oven until crust is golden brown, about 20 minutes, not more.
Remove from heat, allow to cool, and then serve sliced.

Sandwiches:

Hot Sandwich with Mushrooms and Vegan Cheese

Preparation time: 15 minutes

Ingredients for 4 portions:

4 slices of any bread to your liking
5 Portobello mushrooms
1 medium onion, sliced
2 cloves garlic
1 lb. Vegan Mozzarella or any other Vegan cheese to liking
(please find our version of this cheese in the Vegan Cheese Recipes section of this book)
1 tomato, sliced
thyme , dry
2 tbsp. Dijon, to taste
salt and pepper, to taste

Directions:

Sauté mushrooms with onion, garlic, salt, pepper, and thyme. Put Vegan cheese, mushroom mixture, and Dijon mustard on top of 2 slices of bread. Cover with the remaining 2 slices of bread. Put into a preheated to 390°F/200°C oven for 5 minutes. Serve hot.

Hot Sandwich with Zucchini and Tomatoes

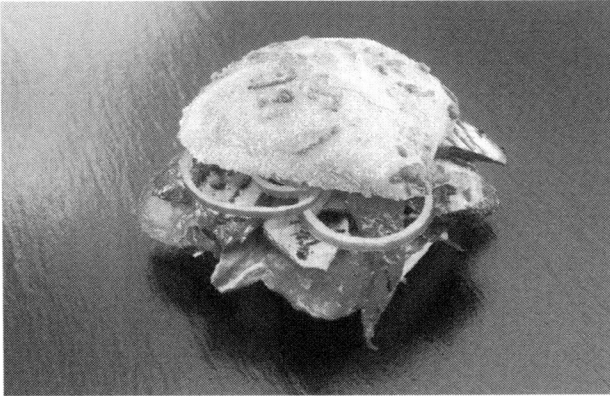

Preparation time: 15 minutes

Ingredients for 4 portions:

4 ciabatta rolls, split, toasted
1 zucchini, cut lengthwise into 6 slices
1 tomato, sliced
Vegan Mozzarella cheese, thinly sliced (please find our version of this cheese in the Vegan Cheese Recipes section of this book)
8 large basil leaves, fresh
1½ table spoon of balsamic vinegar
4 tsp. of olive oil

1/8 tsp. black pepper, freshly ground
salt, to taste

Directions:

Toss zucchini in a bowl with garlic and 2 teaspoons of olive oil. Place zucchini into a grill oven for 2-5 minutes. Remove from grill and sprinkle with vinegar, salt, and pepper. Sprinkle the sliced rolls with olive oil and layer the basil leaves, Vegan Mozzarella cheese, slices of zucchini, tomato, and onion into them. Cover them with the remaining halves of rolls. Heat the sandwiches in an oven and serve hot.

Hot Sandwich with Spinach and Mushrooms

Preparation time: 20 minutes

Ingredients for 4 portions:

4 slices of toasted bread, plain bread, or 4 rolls split in half
10 oz. Portobello mushrooms, cleaned and sliced
2 pinches of fresh spinach, torn or cut
1 bell pepper, sliced
1/2 cup pickled onion

1 clove garlic, minced
1 cup Vegan Almond cheese, shredded (please find our version of this cheese in the Vegan Cheese Recipes section of this book)
cilantro, to taste
1 tbsp. olive oil
salt and pepper, freshly ground
1/4 cup water

Directions:

Cook mushrooms, bell pepper, and olive oil in a frying-pan until soft. Season them with salt, pepper, and garlic. Add spinach and onion and some water, gently tossing the mixture. Add some Vegan Almond cheese and remove from heat. Spread the mixture on bread or 4 halves of rolls, add cilantro and remaining cheese on the top halves of the rolls or remaining bread. Close the rolls and put them into a preheated oven if you like them hot.

Sandwich with Fried Cheese and Salted Green Tomatoes

Preparation time: 15 minutes

Ingredients for 4 portions:

4 rolls, split in half
4 slices Vegan Zucchini grilled cheese (please find our version
of this cheese in the Vegan Cheese recipes section of this
book)
2 green tomatoes, large
1 handful herbs, fresh
1 red onion
5 tbsp. olive oil
salt and pepper, to taste

Directions:

Put the slices of Vegan Zucchini cheese into a grill oven for
less than 2 minutes and then remove. Layer the rolls with
grilled cheese, tomato slices, fresh herbs and onion. Close the
rolls and put them into the grill or bake them for 5 minutes
more if you want to serve them hot.

Sandwich with Rucola and Vegan Mozzarella Cheese

Preparation time: 10 minutes

Ingredients for 4 portions:

8 slices of granary bread
2 oz. rucola, fresh
1/2 red onion, finely sliced
1/2 cup sun-dried tomatoes
3 oz. Vegan Mozzarella cheese, soft finely cut
2 tbsp. olive oil

Directions:
Prepare 4 pieces of bread. Layer the Vegan Mozzarella cheese on top of each. Add seasoning salt, slices of onion, dried tomatoes, and rucola leaves generously. Sprinkle some olive oil on top. Serve cold.

Hamburger with Nut Cutlet

Preparation time: 40 minutes

Ingredients for 4 portions:

For a nut cutlet please see our recipe and ingredients above:

4 rolls, split in half
1 large tomato, sliced
spinach leaves, fresh
salt and pepper, to taste
tomato sauce or ketchup, to taste

Directions:

Prepare 4 rolls cut into 2 flat pieces each. Layer the rolls with spinach leaves, cutlet, and tomato slices. Season with herbs and ketchup if you like. Close the rolls, put them into the grill, and bake for a minute before serving.

25198311R00058

Printed in Poland
by Amazon Fulfillment
Poland Sp. z o.o., Wrocław